IMAGES
of America

FORT LEAVENWORTH

The official crest of the Command and General Staff College was adopted in June 1907. The chevron symbolizes the martial character of the college while the three lamps typify study, learning, and the three branches of the Army—the regular army, the National Guard, and the reserves. The eagle with extended wings symbolizes alertness and sits atop the helmet of a gentleman or esquire. The college's official motto is Ad Bellum Pace Parati (prepared in peace for war). (Courtesy Frontier Army Museum.)

ON THE COVER: Soldiers demonstrate the M1917 Browning machine gun. (Courtesy Frontier Army Museum.)

IMAGES
of America

FORT LEAVENWORTH

All my best

[signature]

Kenneth M. LaMaster

ARCADIA
PUBLISHING

Copyright © 2010 by Kenneth M. LaMaster
ISBN 978-0-7385-6082-3

Published by Arcadia Publishing
Charleston, South Carolina

Printed in the United States of America

Library of Congress Control Number: 2008941581

For all general information contact Arcadia Publishing at:
Telephone 843-853-2070
Fax 843-853-0044
E-mail sales@arcadiapublishing.com
For customer service and orders:
Toll-Free 1-888-313-2665

Visit us on the Internet at www.arcadiapublishing.com

CONTENTS

FOREWORD

I was delighted to be asked to write a brief foreword to Ken LaMaster's latest book on the history of the area he and I have opted to live in. As two who appreciate history, we both find the Leavenworth area a fascinating one. Having lived in the area 32 years, both at Fort Leavenworth and in Leavenworth, I have acquired and read every book I could find about the history of both places. This is the only book I'm aware of that introduces the reader to previously unknown or extremely rare photos of the area and people long passed from the scene. The book covers all aspects of the fort's history, yet it is not a history of the fort, per se. It will certainly introduce the casual reader to the people, famous and forgotten, who added to the fort's glowing history, and to the varying roles the fort played in the development of the West, and its role since 1881 as the premier military educational center of the entire world. It is an all-encompassing, micro-view of a tiny patch of land on the banks of the Missouri River that has left a mark in history much, much larger than its size. LaMaster's interest in and love of the fort is evident in the time and effort he put into researching and writing this valuable addition to our understanding of the role the fort has played since its founding in 1827. I am only saddened by the fact that so many of the earlier members of the Fort Leavenworth Historical Society, of which I am now the longest-serving member, are departed and not here to share my pleasure at having read this book. It isn't a definitive history, but it wasn't intended to be. It certainly accomplishes its purpose of expanding the horizons of we who yearn to learn even more about a fascinating place.

—John Reichley
Leavenworth, Kansas
December 2009
author of *International Officers: A Century of Participation at the United States Army Command and General Staff College* and *The Haunted Hauses of Fort Leavenworth*

ACKNOWLEDGMENTS

First and foremost, I would like to acknowledge and thank the military men and women of Fort Leavenworth. Your dedication and service to your country humbles me. No words I may write or say can ever express the gratitude I have for you and your families.

I would also like to express my gratitude to Steven Allie, Russell Ronspies, and the entire staff of the Frontier Army Museum. Without all of you, this book would have no life. Thanks also to Dr. Marks Gerges, Quentin Schillare, Bob Beardsley, and John C. Webb CSM (Ret) for putting up with all my questions, and the Fort Leavenworth Public Affairs Office for putting up with me while I took photographs. To Jim Will, I am forever indebted to you; your photographs, knowledge, and friendship mean the most. To David R. Phillips, a special thanks for the use of the works of E. E. Henry, R. S. and Horace Stevenson, Horace Putney, and P. L. Huckins. Thanks to the National Archives and Records Administration, Library of Congress, Smithsonian Institute, Combined Arms Research Library, and the Leavenworth Public Library.

To Karen and Brett, I love you both.

I would like to acknowledge and thank Mr. John Reichley, a fellow author and historian, for his assistance with this book. Your knowledge and expertise are what put this project over the top.

INTRODUCTION

Fort Leavenworth, founded in 1827, is the third oldest active military base west of the Mississippi River. Since its humble beginnings as a cantonment established to provide protection for pioneers traveling along the Santa Fe and Oregon Trails, no other military reservation has contributed more to the western expansion of the United States.

Col. Henry Leavenworth, along with 174 men and 13 other officers, established the first campsite along present-day Scott Avenue. In the first few years, those brave soldiers struggled to lay the foundation for a new frontier, as well as the foundation for the future. Their early mission was to inspect cargo being shipped along the Missouri River by keelboat, and to maintain peace among the Native American tribes that populated the area. By the 1830s, the fort provided escorts for doctors to surrounding Native American reservations, aided in the establishment of schools, and expelled squatters on Native American lands. Soldiers also provided provisions and escort for wagon trains traveling along the trade routes into the southwest. Dragoons were outfitted at the fort and patrolled the region, maintaining peace. Col. Stephen W. Kearney left the reservation in 1839 with 10 companies of dragoons on a campaign against the Cherokee—the largest U.S. force ever assembled at that time. By the 1840s, the fort evolved into a major supply depot supplying the forts, posts, and military camps of the West.

When Kansas was established as a territory in 1854, the fort became home to the first territorial capital of Kansas, and the territory's first governor, Andrew Reeder, resided in the quarters known as the Rookery. Built in 1834, the Rookery still stands today as the oldest continually occupied home in Kansas. During the period known as Bleeding Kansas, the soldiers of Fort Leavenworth were heavily involved in the border conflict. At the outbreak of the Civil War, Camp Lincoln was established as a reception center and training station for Kansas volunteers. Fort Sully was established to counter the advance of Confederate forces led by Gen. Sterling Price, who would get turned back by soldiers from the post at the Battle of Westport, securing a legacy that the fort would never come under enemy attack.

On July 17, 1862, Pres. Abraham Lincoln established the first 12 national cemeteries, one of which is located at Fort Leavenworth. This hallowed ground is the final resting place for American heroes dating back to the War of 1812, and is second only to Arlington National Cemetery in the number of Medal of Honor recipients interred there.

In 1866, the U.S. Congress authorized the formation of several black regiments. The 10th U.S. Cavalry was established at the fort under the command of Col. Benjamin Grierson. These brave men, who would become known as Buffalo Soldiers, solidified their place in American military history and are remembered with a monument established in their honor by Gen. Colin Powell when he was the chairman of the Joint Chiefs of Staff.

Between 1865 and 1891, the primary mission of Fort Leavenworth soldiers was to control Native American tribes on the western plains. During this time, the army would engage in combat more than 1,000 times with Native Americans.

The U.S. Disciplinary Barracks (USDB) has operated since 1875 as the military's only long-term maximum-security prison. In 1895, the prison was turned over to the Department of Justice, and operated as the nation's first federal prison until 1906, when it was returned to military control. It remained under military control until 1930, when overcrowded conditions and a riot at the nearby U.S. Penitentiary again returned the USDB to the control of the Department of Justice. It was known as the Federal Prison Annex until 1940. Since then, the USDB has provided inmates with rehabilitation programs and vocational training. Through a vocational trade program, inmates support the Fort Leavenworth Community with a variety of services. A new, state-of-the-art facility was opened in September 2002 on land once occupied by the USDB farm.

In 1881, Gen. William T. Sherman established the School of Application for Cavalry and Infantry—the predecessor to the U.S. Army Command and General Staff College. Fort Leavenworth is the center for excellence in educating officers in leadership development, doctrine, collective training, and battle command. From the school's early doctrine of preparing the army and its leaders for war, to the present-day mission of preparing the army for the Global War on Terrorism and transforming it to meet future threats, the Command and General Staff College is the world leader in professional military education. Its alumni include some of the most recognizable names in military history, for example George S. Patton, Dwight D. Eisenhower, Omar N. Bradley, Colin Powell, Norman Swartzkoff, and David Petreaus. Distinguished instructors have included George C. Marshall, Douglas MacArthur, James Franklin Bell, and Leslie McNair.

Encompassing more than 5,000 acres, Fort Leavenworth is one of the most historic military installations in the country. It was officially designated a National Historic Landmark in 1960. Evolving from its humble beginnings to the present day, military personnel, their families, and civilian employees embrace their place in history forming not only an Army of One, but a Community of One, whose devotion to duty and country is second to none.

One

A NEW FRONTIER

Shortly after the Louisiana Purchase and the expedition of Lewis and Clark, mountain men, pioneers, and fur traders migrated west. After coming under near constant attack by bands of Native Americans, they pleaded for protection. Missouri senator Thomas Hart Benton (right), realizing that the fur trade and trade along the Santa Fe Trail was crucial to the country's expansion westward, argued their case before Congress. Initially it was believed that a fort along the Arkansas River would provide the best protection. Benton persisted that such a fort should instead be established along the Missouri River near the main trade route of the Santa Fe Trail. (Courtesy Library of Congress.)

From late 1825 through most of 1826, Congress debated the establishment of such a fort. By the fall of 1826, Secretary of War James Barbour (left) directed Maj. Gen. Jacob Brown, chief of the U.S. Army (right), to issue orders that would establish a fort for the protection of traders. (Courtesy Library of Congress.)

Order No. 14, dated March 7, 1827, was issued to Col. Henry Leavenworth (left) stating in part: "He will ascend the Missouri River, and when he reaches a point on its left band near the mouth of Little Platte River and within a range of 20 miles above or below its confluence, he will select such position as in his judgment is best calculated for the site of a permanent cantonment." By early April, Colonel Leavenworth, accompanied by Capt. Bennett C. Riley, left Jefferson Barracks ahead of the regiment on a reconnaissance mission in search of such land. (Courtesy Frontier Army Museum.)

Capt. William G. Belknap was in direct command of the 3rd U.S. Infantry when they left Jefferson Barracks on April 17, 1827. Belknap began his military career in 1813 and was twice wounded during the Battle of Niagara. His son William W. Belknap would become Secretary of War in 1869. (Courtesy Library of Congress.)

Colonel Leavenworth instructed his men to establish a temporary camp and construct small huts of hand-hewn logs and slabs of bark. This camp was located on the site of the present-day Main Parade. (Author's collection.)

Several women and children accompanied the men on the initial trip up the Missouri River. Henry J. Hunt was the eight-year-old son of 1st Lt. Samuel Wellington Hunt. Henry would later recall that during the first year, "most of the men were sickly and nearly half the garrison died." Henry J. Hunt would go on to graduate from West Point in 1839. He served in the Mexican War under Gen. Winfield Scott and during the Utah War of 1857. Along with William H. French and William F. Berry, he wrote and published *Instruction for Field Artillery*, a military doctrine considered the bible of field artillery strategy during the Civil War. (Courtesy Library of Congress.)

The men of the 3rd Infantry suffered mostly from malaria and cholera. The outbreaks became so severe at one point that 77 out of the 174 men were sick, and 65 men were enlisted to take care of them. Post medical officer Clement A. Finley (right) issued orders to the men and civilians to stop eating wild berries and melons, believing they were the source of the illnesses. (Courtesy Library of Congress.)

This mural painted by Cpl. E. J. Bransby depicts the early mission of Fort Leavenworth. The duties included the inspection of licenses, cargo hauled by keelboat, and the prevention of alcohol and other contraband into the Indian Territory. (Author's collection.)

In July 1829, Gen. Henry Atkinson (above) ordered Colonel Leavenworth and his men to respond to the only known Native American uprising to occur in the immediate area. Violating a previous treaty, a group of Ioway led by Chief Big Neck returned to their previous hunting grounds along the Chariton River in present-day Kirksville, Missouri. After arguments broke out with nearby settlers, a group of Missouri Militia led by Capt. William Trammell entered the Ioway camp. While negotiations were taking place, the settlers fired on the encampment, killing a woman and her child, and wounding the wife of Chief Big Neck. During the ensuing battle, Captain Trammell was mortally wounded and four others killed. In retaliation for killing the woman and child, the Ioway set fire to all the bodies except that of Captain Trammell, whom they praised for his valor. Chief Big Neck and others were tried and acquitted of murder charges stemming from what many now call the Big Neck War. (Courtesy University of Missouri.)

Under the command of Maj. Bennett C. Riley (right), four companies of troops departed the fort in June 1829. This was the first such mission providing escort for traders along the Santa Fe Trail. It was hoped that such a force would impress on Native Americans that peace was needed along the western frontier. (Courtesy Library of Congress.)

Making the trip in the first caravan were mountain men and fur traders such as Charles Bent (left). The escort accompanied approximately 70 men and 35 wagons to an area along the Arkansas River known as Chouteau's Island. Major Riley's orders were to wait there until the caravans returned in the fall. Bent arraigned for a return escort from Santa Fe by Mexican military forces led by Col. Jose Antonio Viscarra. A meeting and exchange of military courtesies by both forces was held. Charles Bent would establish the largest trading company in the Southwest and was later appointed the first territorial governor of New Mexico. (Author's collection.)

In his official report of the expedition, Lt. Phillip St. George Cooke (left) would write of the meeting between the American and Mexican forces. "No comparable incident is known in early American history. On the common boundary between their respective countries, soldiers of two North American nations paraded before one another in peace, displaying arms and instruction, following which their officers exchanged dinners in accordance with military courtesy. After three days of amenities, the entourage about-faced and arrived at Cantonment Leavenworth on November 8, 1829." (Courtesy Library of Congress.)

Previous caravans of fur traders, mountain men, and pioneers had reported shortages of provisions and Native American attacks along the trail. Many had used horses or mules to pull their wagons. Major Riley had the caravan of 1829 outfitted with oxen. His thought was that as the wagons became lighter, the oxen could provide fresh meat and that they would be less appealing to bands of Native Americans. The oxen performed better than expected and would become the norm for future wagon trains. (Author's collection.)

The original boundaries of Cantonment
Leavenworth were located on land
occupied by the Delaware tribe. The
government and the Delaware negotiated
a treaty on September 24, 1829. Rev. Isaac
McCoy (right), a frontier missionary and
government surveyor, established the
first survey of the military reservation.
In the fall of 1830, McCoy and Delaware
second chief Jonny Quick laid out land
boundaries for the cantonment as well
as lands occupied by the Delaware,
Shawnee, Wyandotte, Pottawatomie,
and Kickapoo tribes. (Courtesy
Combined Arms Research Library.).

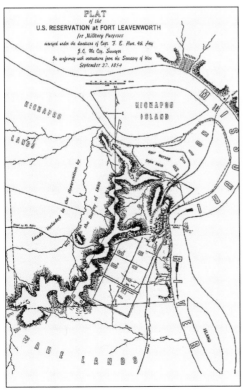

The land survey of 1830 is pictured here.
(Courtesy Combined Arms Research Library.)

Between 1830 and 1834, artist and author George Catlin passed several times through the encampment. Catlin wrote of the fort in 1834 that "the post was garrisoned by six or seven companies with about 15 officers, many whose wives and daughters were present. A dozen white washed cottage-looking houses formed three sides of a hollow square, the fourth being opened and looking over the prairie. It was a hospitable garrison, there was plenty of riding, horseback and carriage, gay parties, picnics to pick strawberries or plums, horse racing, grouse shooting, and deer chasing." (Courtesy Smithsonian Institution.)

In 1833, the great chiefs of the Otoe, Delaware, Shawnee, Peorios, Pawnee, Omaha, Sac, Iowa, Pottawattamie, and Kickapoo tribes all gathered together for talks of peace and a division of tribal areas. Hosted by the U.S. Army, Fort Leavenworth served as a neutral site. The meeting was held under a large gathering of trees on the site of the present-day Main Parade. (Author's collection.)

Two

GATEWAY TO THE WEST

As the nation began to grow and pioneers forged their way west, Fort Leavenworth became the Plymouth Rock to those who would venture forward into the new frontier. Like those who had come to the new world, visions of hope and dreams for a better life began as they stepped from the boats onto the banks of the gateway to the West. The sutler and quartermaster could supply all they would need, but it was the soldiers of Fort Leavenworth who guided the way. Their triumphs and tragedies built the road on which they would travel, faithfully paved by those who would give their all to secure the hopes and dreams of all those who dared to follow. (Author's collection.)

After serving one year as the commander of the first ever battalion of mounted rangers, Maj. Henry Dodge was selected by President Jackson to organize and command the U.S. Regiment of Dragoons, the first mounted unit in the regular army. The newly promoted colonel insisted that Fort Leavenworth be the home of his new regiment, explaining, "This military post presents many advantages. Steamboats could early in the spring bring the necessary supplies to this place. Forage can be procured cheap on the frontier of the state of Missouri and protection would be afforded the inhabitants of this state and would proper point to furnish the necessary escort for the protection of our trade to the Mexican States." (Author's collection.)

Col. Henry Dodge and his regiment of dragoons departed the fort on June 15, 1834, en route to Fort Gibson. There they joined Colonel Leavenworth's group on a mission to negotiate peace with the tribes of the southern plains. From the beginning, the regiment was slowed by intense heat, sickness, and death. Some 500 men began the journey, and by the time they returned 150 had died. Two of the many of the officers who accompanied the expedition were Edwin Vose Sumner (left) and Jefferson Davis (right). (Author's collection.)

Many of the sketches by George Catlin chronicled the expedition in great detail. On July 14, 1834, Colonel Dodge and the regiment encountered the Comanche and were able to establish a hospital at their village to tend to the sick. A treaty could not be negotiated because of the absence of their chief. Colonel Dodge was advised of the location of a tribe of Wichita farther west. (Courtesy Smithsonian Institution.)

While at the Comanche village, Colonel Dodge secured two young girls, a Kiowa about 15 years old, and a Pawnee about 18. Returning the girls to their tribes was thought to be key in the treaty negotiations. (Courtesy Smithsonian Institution.)

On entering the Wichita village, a grand council was arranged. Chiefs and warriors of the Toyash Nation (which included the Pawnee Picts, Wecos, and the Kiowas) were present. During negotiations, Colonel Dodge was able to secure the release of a nine-year-old white boy named Mathew Wright Martin, and the two young girls were reunited with their tribes. The soldiers dined on corn and beans dressed in buffalo fat, watermelon, and plums. Upon his return to Cross Timbers on August 5, Colonel Dodge learned of the death of Colonel Leavenworth. Colonel Dodge would later write, "Perhaps there never has been in America a campaign that operated more severely on man and horses." In military terms, the expedition was a success. (Courtesy Smithsonian Institution.)

On their return to the fort, Colonel Dodge directed the construction of the first brick barracks. These buildings, on the eastern edge of the Main Parade at Sumner Place, housed the first dragoon regiment. Later known as Thomas and McPherson Halls, these buildings would also house officers when the regiment was on campaign. They later housed student officers, departmental headquarters, and the post office before they were torn down in 1903. (Courtesy David R. Phillips.)

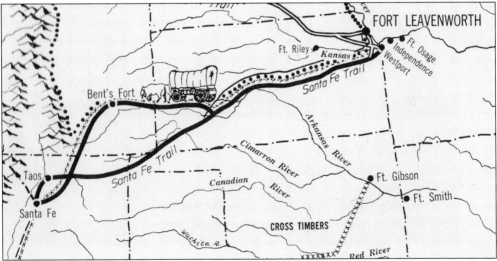

With the establishment of trading posts such as Bent's Fort, further expeditions and wagon trains leaving the fort could travel shorter distances with lighter loads. These outposts could provide provisions and protection along the trail. The expedition of 1835 was the most extensive campaign to date. Departing the fort on May 29, 1835, Colonel Dodge and the Dragoons covered 1,600 miles. Councils were held with the Otoe, Omaha, Arikara, and Arapahoe tribes. At Bent's Fort, Colonel Dodge secured a peace treaty between the bitter enemies the Cheyenne and Pawnee tribes. Most importantly, when the soldiers returned to Fort Leavenworth, every man was reported in good health. (Author's collection.)

In 1836, Col. Steven Watts Kearny (above) assumed command of the 1st Dragoons and was named commander of the Army of the West. Between 1836 and 1841, Colonel Kearny and the regiment patrolled over 1,000 miles of frontier, providing protection for those traveling over the Santa Fe, Oregon, and Utah Trails. Kearny and his men were also detailed with overseeing the moving of more than 37,000 Native Americans from east of the Mississippi, a task carried out by 600 men and officers of his command. The dragoons of Fort Leavenworth were considered the best troops in the army. Colonel Kearny personally negotiated treaties, earning the respect of the chiefs and the nickname *Shonga-Kahega Mahetonga* (Horse Chief of the Long Knives). (Courtesy Library of Congress.)

Under the orders of Colonel Kearny, Capt. James Allen (right) was dispatched to Council Bluffs, Iowa. There he was to raise four or five companies of Mormon men who would be willing to serve their country for 12 months during the War with Mexico. On July 1, 1846, Captain Allen guaranteed "the Mormons would receive rations and other allowances such as volunteers and regular soldiers, they will be afforded all comforts and benefits, and when discharged will be given gratis their arms and accouterments for which they will be fully equipped at Fort Leavenworth." (Courtesy Library of Congress.)

To reassure his followers, Brigham Young (left) followed the remarks of Captain Allen by saying, "Suppose we were admitted into the union as a state and the government did not call on us, we would feel neglected. Let the Mormons be the first to set their feet on the soil of California. Captain Allen has assumed the responsibility of saying that we may locate on Grand Island until we can prosecute our journey. This is the first offer we have ever had from the government to benefit us." (Library of Congress.)

James. S. Brown (left) wrote in his autobiography *Life of a Pioneer*, "The place being an outfitting station for the U.S. forces in the War with Mexico, all was bustle with activity; steamboats unloading material, and teams filled the streets; many of the new recruits were very rough indeed, drinking and fighting seemed to be their pastime; myself and companions were amazed and shocked at the profane and vulgar language and vile actions we were compelled to listen to and witness; with all else, squads of soldiers being drilled, the bugle sound was frequent as were the beating of the drum and playing of the fife, everywhere men were preparing for victory or death, and many were so reckless they did not seem to care which came." (Courtesy American Libraries Internet Archive.)

On August 10, 1846, Companies A, B, and C moved out, followed a few days later by companies D and E. Newly promoted Lt. Col. James Allen took ill and temporarily placed Capt. Jefferson Hunt of Company A in command. Captain Allen returned to the garrison, where he passed away on August 23. Lt. Col. A. J. Smith (right) assumed command, and was later replaced by Lt. Col. Phillip St. George Cooke. (Courtesy Library of Congress.)

As the War with Mexico became imminent, Col. Alexander W. Doniphan (right) reported to the fort along with the 856 men of the 1st Regiment Missouri Mounted Volunteers. With a force of nearly 1,700 men, 12 six-pound, and 4 twelve-pound howitzers, Colonel Kearny departed the garrison en route to Bent's Fort from where the invasion of New Mexico began on August 12, 1846. (Author's collection.)

Kearny's forces entered the town of Las Vegas, New Mexico, on August 15, 1846, meeting almost no resistance along the way. This engraving depicts Colonel Kearny's proclamation of New Mexico as part of the United States. By September, a civilian government was in place and Charles Bent was appointed governor of the territory. On September 25, 1846, Kearny departed for California along with 300 men. Along the way, the dragoons were victorious at the Battle of San Pasqual. Combining with naval forces under the command of Commodore Robert F. Stockton, the U.S. Army defeated the Californios and signed the treaty of Cahuenga on January 13, 1847. Kearny assumed the duties as the military governor of the California Territory. (Courtesy Library of Congress.)

Col. Sterling Price (above), leading the 2nd Regiment of Missouri Mounted Cavalry, assumed command of the Territory of New Mexico once Colonel Kearny and the Dragoons departed for California. Many of the New Mexicans feared U.S. forces would not honor land titles issued by the Mexican government, and rumors of a revolt began to surface. On January 19, 1847, the revolt broke out when a band of insurgents attacked the home of Gov. Charles Bent, killing him and several other government officials. Price, along with 300 Missouri volunteers and 65 locals, defeated a force of nearly 1,500 insurgents at the Battles of Santa Cruz de la Canada and Embudo Pass. Price's official report surmised, "It appeared to be the object of the insurgents to put to death every man who had accepted office under the American government." (Courtesy Missouri Historical Society.)

Three

PHOTOGRAPHS AND MEMORIES

Francis Parkman wrote: "On the next morning we rode to Fort Leavenworth. Colonel, now General Kearney, to whom I had the honor of an introduction when at St. Louis, just arrived and received us at his headquarters with the highbred courtesy habitual to him. Fort Leavenworth is in fact no fort, being without defensive works, except two blockhouses. No rumors of war had as yet disturbed its tranquility. In the square grassy area, surrounded by barracks and quarters for officers, the men were passing and re-passing, or lounging among the trees." (Courtesy Kansas Historical Society.)

The Rookery was built around 1834. Constructed of stone and hand-hewn timbers, this residence is the oldest continually occupied home in the state of Kansas. In 1879, a brick extension was added and the building was later stuccoed. Listed on the register for historic places, this building underwent renovation in 2009, remaining true to its original construction. It stands ready to welcome military families and their guests for generations to come. (Courtesy Library of Congress.)

Legends persist that some of the old homes and buildings of the fort are haunted. The Rookery, whose foyer is shown here c. 1985, has its stories. There are reports of a young woman with scraggly hair and long fingernails moving about the house in a long white flowing gown. A young girl saw a pale woman and child asking for help. A colonel's wife felt a shove while carrying things to the basement, but invisible hands broke her fall. (Courtesy Library of Congress.)

This sketch by H. W. Waugh depicts the early days of Fort Leavenworth. Many wives and families accompanied the officers and men during their campaigns across the plains. As the post grew, many officers and their units took up winter quarters on the reservation. Many kept diaries recounting the early days on the small frontier post. (Courtesy Frontier Army Museum.)

By the early 1850s, westward expansion was at a fever pitch. The post began outfitting survey crews that were dispatched to establish the most economical routes for a railroad system, military roads, and smaller military outpost. By 1853, Col. T. Fauntleroy suggested it would be in the best interest of the military to abandon the post for a more central location in Kansas. Secretary of War Jefferson Davis disagreed, declaring, "The convenience of the fort to the Missouri River, especially since no railroads have yet reached into Kansas, makes retention of the post desirable." The above photograph was taken at the corner of present-day McPherson and McClelland Avenues. (Courtesy Frontier Army Museum.)

In 1855, Erasmus T. Carr (left) was living in St. Paul, Minnesota, when a letter arrived from a friend. He was advised that Colonel Sumner was in Syracuse, New York, looking for 50 carpenters for the reconstruction of the post. Arriving at the post landing September 14, 1855, Carr wrote, "Where is the fort, so far we have seen nothing but the warehouse and landing, with our traps loaded we followed the teams to the top of the hill, there we found quite a group of buildings, few detached, a greater number built about a square. Built of stone, brick, logs and frame, a number of half tumbled down shacks." Still the question, "where's the fort?" (Courtesy Kansas Historical Society.)

Located just north of Sumner Place was this one-story brick and stone building. It served as an assembly hall, school, and post chapel. From October 7 to November 24, 1854, it also served as the first territorial capital of Kansas. (Courtesy Frontier Army Museum.)

The passing of the Kansas-Nebraska Act of 1854 repealed the Missouri Compromise of 1820, opening new land and allowing settlers of those lands to determine if they would allow slavery within their boundaries. One such family was that of William "Buffalo Bill" Cody, who moved to the nearby Salt Creek Valley area. Isaac Cody, Buffalo Bill's father, spoke out openly against slavery. During one such speech, he enraged pro-slavery advocates, who mobbed and stabbed him. Isaac Cody would later die of the injuries received that day. (Courtesy Kansas Historical Society.)

On June 29, 1854, Pres. Franklin Pierce appointed Andrew Reeder (left) governor of the Territory of Kansas. Reeder established offices at the fort, resided in the Rookery, and took his meals with the post sutler. For the next several months, tensions increased between pro-slavery Missouri and anti-slavery Kansas. On March 30, 1855, violence erupted after Missourians illegally voted in Kansas, causing one of the largest cases of voter fraud in U.S. history, and a border war commonly referred to as Bleeding Kansas. (Courtesy Kansas State Historical Society.)

Designed and built by E. T. Carr in 1855 and 1856, these double sets of officers' quarters are called Syracuse houses after Carr's hometown of Syracuse, New York. Each set of quarters was designed to house four captains. Another set of these homes was also built at the same time but both were destroyed by fire in 1890. (Courtesy Frontier Army Museum.)

A letter written by Capt. George D. Bayard (left) described the holiday season of 1856: "I have enjoyed myself during the holidays very well. There were two balls in Leavenworth City, one at Planters House, the other McCracken's Hotel. The former pro-slavery, the latter free state. Most of the officers went to both, but as all my lady acquaintances was at Planters House I remained there. I am told that even at Planters House there were more free-state ladies than there were pro-slavery ladies." (Courtesy Library of Congress.)

As westward expansion escalated, the army realized it did not have the resources available at Fort Leavenworth to adequately transport the volume of supplies needed. The army awarded a two-year contract to the freighting company of Russell, Majors, and Waddell, which employed nearly 1,700 men and owned 7,500 head of oxen and 500 wagons. During the summer of 1857, they outlined 48 wagon trains hauling almost 4 tons of goods from Fort Leavenworth. (Author's collection.)

In the summer of 1857, eight companies of cavalry left the fort under the command of Colonel Sumner on a mission to intercept the Cheyenne, who were attacking and destroying wagon trains along the prairie. On July 18, Col. Edmund Alexander's detachment left for the Utah Territory, and was later met by the detachment of Col. Albert Sidney Johnson (right). The Utah War was an armed dispute between the Mormon settlers of Utah and the federal government. Though called a war, there were no actual battles, and peace was achieved through negotiations. (Author's collection.)

In 1858, the Secretary of War directed that an Ordnance Depot be established at the post that would take the place of the one located at Liberty Landing, Missouri. This arsenal would be comprised of 138 acres located along the southeastern edge of the post. E. T. Carr oversaw the design and construction of the arsenal facilities. (Courtesy Frontier Army Museum.)

During the Mexican War, an ordnance depot had been located in the old headquarters building with the magazine (left) being located below ground at the center of the Main Parade. (Courtesy Frontier Army Museum.)

This area of the arsenal was located at the corner of Gibbons and Meade. The buildings pictured here are, from left to right, Stotsenburg Hall, the arsenal fire station, and little beehive. (Courtesy Frontier Army Museum.)

Sherman Hall (above) and Wagner Hall were originally built in the 1860s as a storehouse and offices for the arsenal. (Courtesy Frontier Army Museum.)

This view shows the arsenal, including the vineyard. (Courtesy Frontier Army Museum.)

The arsenal commander's residence was located at the corner of Augur and Scott Avenues. Built on the site of the original soldiers' cemetery, this residence now serves as the home of the post commander. (Courtesy Frontier Army Museum.)

These houses were located to the south and east of the arsenal. The outline of Wagner Hall can be seen to the right the structures. (Courtesy Frontier Army Museum.)

A view from the arsenal grounds shows the military prison. (Courtesy Frontier Army Museum.)

On the evening of July 23, 1870, one of the most tragic events in Fort Leavenworth's history occurred at the arsenal. Bvt. Col. David H. Buell (above), arsenal commander, was escorting his wife and son home after an evening at the home of General Sturgis. At approximately 11:00 p.m., as the family entered the gate of their quarters, a shot rang out. The bullet struck Colonel Buell in the chest, killing him instantly. The assailant fled but was later identified as John M. Malone, who had worked as an orderly to Colonel Buell. He had recently deserted after being reprimanded for drunkenness while on duty. The officers of the fort collected $500 as a bounty for Malone. A few days later, Malone entered the home of a Mr. Creemer, the arsenal engineer, and demanded money. A sentry spotted Malone, who then ran toward the Missouri River. After securing a raft to ferry him across the river, he made his way to Weston, Missouri, where he was recognized and confronted by a mob. During a struggle, Malone's rifle discharged, mortally wounding him. Before his passing, Malone confessed to the murder. He also implicated a gambler named Ackley as an accomplice, accusing him of having conspired to the murder and providing the weapon used. (Author's collection.)

Four

A NATION DIVIDED, A POST UNITED

In the early days of the Civil War, Confederate officers drew up plans to attack all the small posts along the western frontier, cutting off communication with Federal forces. Once accomplished, they would turn their attention to Fort Leavenworth, where the arsenal held large quantities of ordnance, guns, small arms, and equipment. Brig. Gen. William S. Harney (right), realizing the small number of troops garrisoned at the post would be little resistance to such a force, ordered two companies each of artillery and infantry as reinforcements. (Courtesy National Archives and Records Administration.)

The ordnance depot at Liberty, Missouri, was broken into on April 20, 1861. Citizens of Leavenworth, fearing an attack on the fort was forthcoming, offered 100 men to Capt. William Steele (left) to aid in the defense of the arsenal. Just over a month later, Captain Steele would resign his U.S. Army commission, taking up the cause of the Confederacy as a colonel in the 7th Texas Cavalry. (Author's collection.)

Capt. Jesse Lee Reno (right) assumed command of the arsenal and immediately called on the governor of Kansas to assist in the defense of the fort until the arrival of Col. Nelson A. Miles and reinforcements. Shortly thereafter, Captain Reno would be promoted to brigadier general and take command of the 2nd Brigade IX Corps of Virginia Volunteers. On September 12, 1862, a Confederate sharpshooter killed Brigadier General Reno as he led his troops at the Battle of South Mountain. (Courtesy Library of Congress.)

Responding to Captain Reno, the governor of Kansas called on Leavenworth City to form three volunteer companies of militia. The Leavenworth Light Infantry commanded by Capt. Powell Clayton (right) mustered in on April 29, and on June 3, 1861, was mustered into Federal service as part of the 1st Kansas Infantry. (Courtesy Library of Congress.)

Capt. Edward Cozzens (left) commanded the Union Guard mustering in at the fort. Cozzens would muster into Federal service, and he saw action at Wilson's Creek, Yorktown, Williamsburg, Fair Oaks, Gaines Mills, Malvern Hill, Antietam, Fredericksburg, Gettysburg, and the Wilderness. (Courtesy Library of Congress.)

The Shields Guards mustered in under the command of Capt. Daniel McCook (left). McCook had been practicing law in Leavenworth and was a partner of William T. Sherman. He would remain with the 1st Kansas Volunteers and see action in southwest Missouri. Commissioned colonel of the 52nd Ohio Volunteer Infantry, he saw action at Lexington, Louisville, and Nashville. He would succumb to injuries received at the Battle of Kennesaw Mountain on July 27, 1864. General McCook was the son of Maj. Daniel McCook, brother of Charles and Robert McCook, all of whom perished of battlefield injuries during the Civil War. (Courtesy Library of Congress.)

After being routed at the First Battle of Bull Run on July 21, 1861, a special war council was convened in Washington, D.C. General of the Army Winfield Scott (right) insisted that the government could not protect the east and the western territories with the troops available. He recommended all troops be recalled from the West and all military posts be abandoned. (Courtesy Library of Congress.)

The council of war (right) took the recommendation of General Scott, issuing the order to recall all troops of the West and abandon all military reservations. Alexander Caldwell was an influential businessman who had contracts to move military supplies throughout the western territories. He traveled to Washington, and petitioned his friends (including the Assistant Secretary of War) into maintaining all interest in the West and to increase the number of troops garrisoned at Fort Leavenworth. (Courtesy Kansas Historical Society.)

James Henry Lane (left) came to Kansas in 1855 and became involved in the abolitionist movement. Lane formed the Kansas Brigade at the fort during the Civil War. After their defeat at the Battle of Dry Wood Creek, the brigade began raiding and pillaging Missouri border towns. Nicknamed "Red Legs" because of the red leggings they wore, the brigade entered the town of Osceola, Missouri, on September 23, 1861, burned it to the ground, and murdered nine men. The sacking of Osceola by Lane's Red Legs would become the basis for the movie *The Outlaw Josie Wales*. (Courtesy Library of Congress.)

Two of the most prominent figures mustering into service at the fort were James Butler Hickok (left) and William Cody. Hickok served with Lanes "Red Legs" and later served as a spy under Gen. Samuel R. Curtis reporting the movement of Confederate forces throughout Arkansas, Missouri, and Kansas. Cody mustered into service with the 7th Kansas Calvary serving as a teamster. Cody would also serve as a scout and dispatch bearer for Gen. William Tecumseh Sherman. (Author's collection.)

With the many men who would be mustering into service at the fort, an area named Camp Lincoln was established for the outfitting and training of those units. Above is a light battery at Camp Lincoln. (Courtesy Frontier Army Museum.)

INDEPENDENT
KANSAS
Jay-Hawkers.

Volunteers are wanted for the 1st Regiment of Ka
sas Volunteer Cavalry to serve our country

During the War.

Horses will be furnished by the Government. Go
horses will be purchased of the owner who voluntee
Each man will be mounted, and armed with a Shar
Rifle, a Navy Revolver, and a Sabre. The pay will
that of the regular volunteer.

Volunteers from Northern Kansas will rendezvo
at Leavenworth. Those from Southern Kans
will rendezvous at Mound City. Volunteers sing
parts of companies and full companies will be must
ed into the United States service as soon as they rep
themselves to the local recruiting officer at either of t
above places. Upon arriving at Mound City voluntee
will report themselves to John T. Snoddy, Acting A
jutant. Those who rendezvous at Leavenworth w
report themselves to D. R. Anthony, Esq. of that pla
C. R. JENNISON,
Col. 1st Regiment Kansas Vol. Cavalry
MOUND CITY, Aug. 24, 1861.

Charles R. "Doc" Jennison (above) received a commission of colonel from Kansas governor Charles L. Robinson and mustered the 7th Kansas Cavalry in at Fort Leavenworth on October 28, 1861. The regiment would become known as Jennison's Jayhawkers, and it patrolled the border between Kansas and Missouri. Jennison temporarily resigned his commission in April 1862, after Maj. Gen. James G. Blunt was given command of the Department and Army of Kansas. In 1864, Doc Jennison was reinstated as colonel and given command of the 15th Kansas Cavalry. Colonel Jennison's brigade aided in the defeat of Gen. Sterling Price during Price's raid of October 1864. Shortly thereafter, Jennison was arrested, court-martialed, and convicted of his wartime crimes. He received a dishonorable discharge. (Courtesy Kansas Historical Society.)

On December 31, 1863, Secretary of War Edwin McMasters Stanton (left) established the Department of Kansas under the command of Gen. Samuel R. Curtis (right) with headquarters at Fort Leavenworth. Curtis was in command of training at Jefferson Barracks, Camp Benton, and the defenses of St. Louis. His forces were responsible for repelling Sterling Price's from Missouri and winning the Battles of Big Sugar Creek and Pea Ridge. (Courtesy Library of Congress.)

In September 1864, Gen. Sterling Price again was set to attack Fort Leavenworth with an estimated 20,000 Confederate forces. At the urging of General Curtis, Kansas governor Thomas Carney (left) issued a call for the militia, entreating, "Men of Kansas, Rally! One blow, one earnest, united blow, will foil the invader and save you. Who will falter? Who is not ready to meet the peril? Who will not defend his home and the state?" (Courtesy Kansas Historical Society.)

Maj. Gen. George W. Dietzler (right) was placed in command of the Kansas State Militia. Dietzler had helped organize the 1st Kansas Volunteers and was wounded in the Battle of Wilson's Creek. Dietzler commanded troops that formed the right flank of Gen. James Blunt's forces during the Battle of Westport. (Courtesy Kansas State Historical Society.)

Gen. Thomas A. Davies (left) was placed in command of the defenses of the fort along with Maj. Franklin E. Hunt, who was in command of the defense of Leavenworth City. A series of earthworks (right) were established along the southwestern edge of the fort overlooking the city. Siege guns were placed high upon a ridge overlooking the area and named Fort Sully. A line of earthworks was dug in the city along Michigan Avenue. (Author's collection.)

James G. Blunt was appointed as lieutenant colonel of the 2nd Kansas Volunteer Regiment in 1861. In 1862, Blunt was promoted to the grade of brigadier general and given command of the Department and Army of Kansas. His forces were defeated at the first Battle of Newtonia but saw victories at the Battles of Old Fort Wayne and Prairie Grove. While transferring command of the District of the Frontier from Fort Scott to Fort Smith, his troops came under attack by forces led by William C. Quantrill. In 1864, Blunt was given command of the 1st Division of the Army of the Border. He engaged Price's Confederates at the Battle of Lexington, Missouri, and again at the Little Blue River. Blunt established a defensive stronghold with three brigades along Brush Creek. The Battle of Westport was one of the largest battles west of the Mississippi River with over 30,000 troops and 3,000 casualties. With the defeat of General Price's Confederate forces, Missouri was now under Union control. (Courtesy Kansas Historical Society.)

Five

BUFFALO SOLDIER

On August 4, 1862, Kansas senator James H. Lane ordered Capt. James M. Williams' 5th Kansas Cavalry to begin recruiting and organizing a regiment of infantry composed of African American men. Orders called for the procurement of supplies and establishment of a camp for rendezvous and instruction near Fort Leavenworth. Within 60 days, 500 men had been recruited and formed the 1st Kansas Colored Regiment. The regiment engaged in the Battles of Island Mound, Reeder Farm, Cabin Creek, Honey Springs, Poison Springs, Flat Rock Creek, and Timber Hills. Above is the banner of Company F 1st Kansas Colored Volunteer Infantry. (Courtesy Kansas Historical Society.)

After enduring the prejudice of several civilians, including an attempt to arrest the men and officers by civil authorities, the regiment was mobilized and ordered to proceed to Bates County, Missouri. On October 27, 1862, the first Kansas Colored Regiment came under attack by the Missouri State Guard and guerrillas. Although outnumbered, the regiment battled for two days, and forced the defeat and retreat of the guerrillas. Known as the Skirmish at Island Mound, the incident was reported in newspapers all over the country and was the first battle of the Civil War in which an African American regiment was engaged. (Courtesy Library of Congress.)

One of the bloodiest engagements involving the 1st Kansas Colored occurred at Poison Spring on April 18, 1864, during the Camden Expedition. Confederate forces led by Brig. Gens. J. S. Marmaduke and S. B. Maxey attacked, killing more than 300 men. Their captors murdered most of the 1st Kansas Colored who were wounded or captured. "Remember Poison Spring!" became the battle cry. (Courtesy Library of Congress.)

In June 1863, Col. Thomas J. Anderson (left) began recruiting for the 2nd Kansas Colored Volunteer Infantry. Between August and October of 1863, companies were mustered into service, and on November 1, the regiment was formed under the command of Col. S. J. Crawford (right). The 2nd Kansas would win a decisive battle over Watie's guerrillas at Iron Bridge. In the summer of 1864, the 1st Kansas became the 79th and the 2nd Kansas became the 83rd U.S. Colored Infantries. The units mustered out of service October 1 and October 9, 1865. (Courtesy Library of Congress.)

On June 29, 1864, General Curtis sought and was granted permission to form a light artillery battery of "Negro descent and commanded by Negro officers." Maj. Richard Hunt was chief of artillery and placed Lt. William D. Mathews (right) in charge of recruitment. Lt. Mathews' commission would come under fire but would be upheld after 21 white officers sent a letter to Senator Lane explaining, "Lt. Mathews is among the most thorough and efficient officers in our organization; a soldier in every sense of term, drilled, disciplined, and capable." (Courtesy Kansas Historical Society.)

As the army of Gen. Sterling Price advanced in October 1864, the five companies of African American light artillery and militia had been established. One company set up defensive positions on the ridge overlooking Fort Sully. Other companies of the battery fought in the Battles of the Blue and Westport alongside General Blunt's forces and helped defeat Price's forces at the Battle of Mine Creek. Secretary of War Edwin Stanton designated this unit an independent battery and named the unit the Douglas Battery in honor of Capt. H. Ford Douglas who had assumed command of the unit in February 1865. The unit was mustered out of service at Fort Leavenworth on July 22, 1865. (Courtesy Frontier Army Museum.)

As the U.S. Army reorganized after the Civil War, Congress passed legislation creating six all–African American units—the 9th and 10th U.S. Cavalry and the 38th, 39th, 40th, and 41st Infantry Regiments. On September 21, 1866, the U.S. 10th Cavalry Regiment was formed at Fort Leavenworth and was commanded by Col. Benjamin H. Grierson (left). Grierson set high standards of recruitment and by the end of July 1867, eight companies of enlisted men had been recruited. (Courtesy Library of Congress.)

Colonel Grierson's orders to Capt. L. H. Carpenter stated, "Recruit men sufficiently educated to fill positions of noncommissioned officers, clerks, and mechanics in the regiment. You will use the greatest of care in your selection of recruits. Enlist all the superior men you can who will bring a credit to the regiment." Little did the colonel know that these men, who would become known as Buffalo Soldiers, would distinguish themselves as one of the most elite cavalry units in U.S. Army history. (Courtesy David R. Phillips.)

The company mottoes of the 9th and 10th U.S. Cavalry are pictured here. (Author's collection.)

From 1866 to 1888, Colonel Grierson's soldiers, such as James Satchell (seated) and Samuel Pipton (standing), served distinctively in the cavalry on the Plains in skirmishes with Native Americans in places such as Beecher Island, eastern Colorado, and Beaver Creek. After building Fort Sill, the unit was transferred to the Department of Texas to explore and survey. Along the way, it gained the respect of Native American tribes, who gave the black soldier the nickname "Buffalo Soldiers" for their tenacity and fearless fighting ability. (Courtesy Frontier Army Museum.)

As their legend grew, artists of the time such as Frederic Remington used pen and ink to record life as a Buffalo Soldier. The drawings were printed in such magazines as *Harper's Weekly*, *Leslies Illustrated*, and *Collier's*. (Courtesy Library of Congress.)

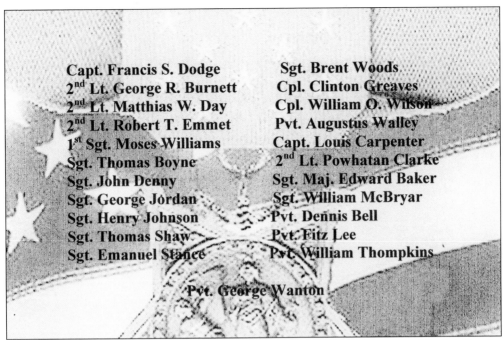

Capt. Francis S. Dodge
2nd Lt. George R. Burnett
2nd Lt. Matthias W. Day
2nd Lt. Robert T. Emmet
1st Sgt. Moses Williams
Sgt. Thomas Boyne
Sgt. John Denny
Sgt. George Jordan
Sgt. Henry Johnson
Sgt. Thomas Shaw
Sgt. Emanuel Stance

Sgt. Brent Woods
Cpl. Clinton Greaves
Cpl. William O. Wilson
Pvt. Augustus Walley
Capt. Louis Carpenter
2nd Lt. Powhatan Clarke
Sgt. Maj. Edward Baker
Sgt. William McBryar
Pvt. Dennis Bell
Pvt. Fitz Lee
Pvt. William Thompkins

Pvt. George Wanton

On September 18, 1879, after five days of tracking the Apache chief Victorio, men of the 9th Cavalry were ambushed at Las Animas Canyon, New Mexico. Seeing a wounded soldier approximately 100 yards away, Sgt. John Denny disobeyed orders, ran the distance under heavy fire, put the soldier on his back, and carried him to safety. For his bravery under fire, Denny received the Medal of Honor. Above is a roll call of the 23 members of the 9th and 10th Cavalry who received the Medal of Honor for their brave and heroic acts. (Author's collection.)

After 32 years of patrolling the West, the men of the 9th and 10th would again distinguish themselves in battle, this time on foreign soil. Under the command of Gen. Joseph Wheeler, the Buffalo Soldiers departed from Tampa, Florida, on June 14, 1898, sailing for Cuba and the Spanish-American War. (Courtesy Combined Arms Research Library.)

Members of the 10th U.S. Cavalry are pictured advancing on the Spanish at the Battle of Las Guasimas on June 24, 1898. (Courtesy Library of Congress.)

On July 1, 1898, some 13,000 troops—including 2,000 Buffalo Soldiers—engaged the enemy at the Battles of El Caney and San Juan Hill. Teddy Roosevelt's rough riders have been credited with winning the Battle of San Juan Hill, but many historians now believe that the men of the 10th U.S. Cavalry engaged the enemy that day and that the rough riders had actually engaged the enemy at the Battle of Kettle Hill. In his *New York Times* article of July 6, 1898, Timothy Egan wrote, "Regulars and volunteers, blacks and whites, fought side by side, endured the blistering heat and driving rain, and shared food and drink as well as peril and discomfort. They forged a victory that did not belong primarily to TR, nor did it belong to the Buffalo Soldiers. It belonged to all of them." (Courtesy Library of Congress.)

Addressing the troops on September 7, 1898, Gen. Joseph Wheeler said: "The valor displayed by you was not without sacrifice. Eighteen percent, or nearly one in five, of the cavalry division fell on the field either killed or wounded. We mourn the loss of these heroic dead, and a grateful country will always revere their memory. Whatever may be my fate, wherever my steps may lead, my heart will always burn with increasing admiration for your courage in action." (Courtesy Frontier Army Museum.)

After the Spanish-American War, different elements of the Buffalo Soldiers were assigned along the border of Mexico, Vancouver Barracks, and the Philippines. A detachment of the 9th was garrisoned at Fort Leavenworth from the early 1900s, followed by a detachment of the 10th from 1931 to 1944. The photograph below shows members of Troop F, 9th Cavalry outside their riding hall, now known as Gruber Fitness Center. (Courtesy Frontier Army Museum.)

While stationed at the fort from 1981 to 1982, Gen. Colin Powell discovered that no lasting memory existed of the brave and courageous Buffalo Soldiers. With the help of Brig. Gen. Alonzo Dougherty Jr., U.S. Navy Comdr. Carlton G. Philpot, the Buffalo Soldiers Committee, artist Lee W. Brubaker, and sculptor Eddie Dixon, fund-raisers, grants, and donations were collected. On July 28, 1990, General Powell, the chairman of the Joint Chiefs of Staff, dedicated the 12-foot-9-inch-tall bronze statue, quoting the last order of Col. Benjamin H. Grierson. "The officers and enlisted men have cheerfully endured many hardships and privations, and in the midst of great dangers steadfastly maintained a most gallant and zealous devotion to duty. They may well be proud of the record made, and rest assured that the hard work undergone in the accomplishment of such valuable service to their country cannot fail, sooner or later, to meet with due recognition and reward." (Author's collection.)

Six

FOR GOD AND COUNTRY

Though there was a demand among soldiers and civilians alike, Congress did not approve the employment of chaplains until the army's reorganization of 1838. Prior to that, it is believed that many missionaries among the Native American tribes tended to the spiritual needs of those early settlers of Fort Leavenworth. Men of faith, such as Baptist missionary Isaac McCoy, conducted services prior to 1831. Fr. Pierre-Jean De Smet (right) came west in 1831 and is credited with holding some of the first organized services in the area. Records indicate that the first marriage recorded at the fort was that of Lt. Oliver D. Green to Kate Rich on October 6, 1859. Rich was the daughter of post trader Hiram Rich. Lt. Oliver D. Green later became adjutant general and a Medal of Honor recipient. (Courtesy Library of Congress.)

Shortly after his arrival in 1833, Rev. Jerome C. Berryman wrote this account of his experiences: "It did not take me long to have some log cabin buildings erected for my family, and a schoolhouse of the same sort in which to open a school, and by midwinter I had about 90 children in attendance. Here for eight consecutive years with my faithful wife and other helpers, I labored in teaching the young and old, often preaching to the soldiers of the fort, and also frequently visiting and helping at other mission stations among the Shawnee, Delaware, Peoria, and Pottawatomie." (Courtesy Iron County Historical Society.)

Construction began on the Memorial Chapel (below) in 1878 under the authority of Gen. John Pope, with inmates from the military prison providing the labor. Its cornerstone was laid during services on Easter morning May 5, 1878, with the dedication ceremony on November 28, 1878. The first baptism took place on January 22, 1879, when George and Emma Ashman's daughter Ida was four months old. The first wedding was that of Sidney Hayden Jr. to Mary Walker on June 3, 1879. (Courtesy Frontier Army Museum.)

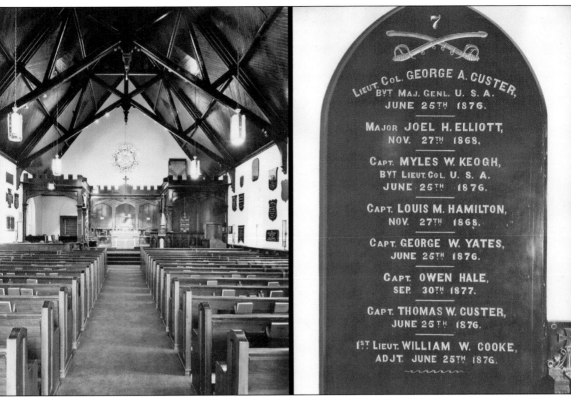

The interior of the chapel is adorned with tablets memorializing deceased officers and enlisted men. Among the first tablets placed were those commemorating the men who lost their lives during the Battle of Little Big Horn. The congregation as well as many officers and enlisted men who served previously at Fort Leavenworth answered the call for donations for the church organ, which was called the Sherman-Sheridan Memorial Organ. It was manufactured by the Carl Barchoff Church Organ Company and is 8 feet wide, 5 feet deep, and about 15 feet high. (Courtesy Frontier Army Museum.)

Prior to 1870, a one-story building that had been previously used to house members of the 7th cavalry was used for Catholic services. Many parishioners appealed to Bishop John B. Miege (left) to apply to the Secretary of War for a new building. One such appeal written by Gen. Michael R. Morgan read, "This temporary chapel was also used by the regimental band at the post for practice. It was found that the band spilled their beer over the altar and that they entered the recess back of the altar used as the sacristy and disturbed what they found there. It is thought that this could easiest be amended by the Catholics putting up their own church edifice." (Courtesy Library of Congress.)

On approval, Gen. Michael R. Morgan and Ordnance Sgt. Cornelius Kelly began raising funds for the construction. The cornerstone of the first St. Ignatius Chapel was set in 1871. Legend states that a rectory building adjacent the chapel was destroyed by fire in 1875, claiming the life of a young priest known as Father Fred. Materials that were salvaged from the fire were purportedly used to build a house on the site of the old rectory. Many have claimed to see Father Fred walking the home in his priestly robes. (Courtesy Frontier Army Museum.)

Between September 1885 and June 1889, the Diocese of Leavenworth and the Secretary of War negotiated terms for the new St. Ignatius Chapel. The details included a tract of land measuring 200 square feet. The church edifice would not exceed 45-by-95 feet. The agreement also included a schoolhouse measuring 25-by-50 feet. The church was to be Gothic design that included a rectory and eight rooms, with a large hall for church functions in the basement. Bishop Louis Maria Fink laid the cornerstone of the church on August 18, 1889. (Courtesy Frontier Army Museum.)

An interior view of St. Ignatius Chapel shows the altar. Stained-glass panels were donated during the construction and were dedicated to the memories of Bishop Miege, Ellen Ewing Sherman, Gen. Phillip Sheridan, and Lieutenant Colonel Brotherton. (Courtesy Frontier Army Museum.)

On December 16, 2001, an electrical fire destroyed the 112-year-old St. Ignatius Chapel. A park now stands where the chapel once stood. (Courtesy *The Fort Leavenworth Lamp*.)

On July 17, 1862, Congress enacted legislation enabling the president to purchase lands for the establishment of national cemeteries. Fort Leavenworth was designated one of the first 14 sites for a national cemetery in the country. Prior to its establishment, remains were buried according to military tradition. Enlisted men were interred on a site that now includes the post commander's residence, while the officers were interred on grounds that included the Combined Arms Research Library. (Courtesy Frontier Army Museum.)

The oldest known burial at the fort is that of Clarinda Dale, who died September 21, 1844. The oldest known military grave is that of Capt. James Allen of the 1st U.S. Dragoons of the Mormon Battalion, who died in August 1846. (Author's collection.)

This cannon sat in the cemetery for many years. The bronze plaque affixed read, "United States National Military Cemetery Fort Leavenworth, Established 1861, Interments 1341, Known 597, Unknown 744." (Courtesy Frontier Army Museum.)

JAMES CALHOUN

1 LIEUT   CAVALRY

INDIAN WAR

JUNE 25 1876

7TH US CAVALRY

THOMAS W CUSTER

2 MEDALS OF HONOR

CAPT CO C

7 OHIO CAV.

JUNE 25 1876

From the writings of post chaplain Hiram Stone, "On Friday evening of August 3, 1877, at the post chapel and at the military cemetery at Fort Leavenworth, I performed services at the interment of the following officers of the 7th U.S. Cavalry who were in an engagement with hostile members of the Sioux tribe at the Little Big Horn River in the territory of Montana on the 25th day of June 1876: Capt. George W. Yates, Capt. Thomas W. Custer, 1st Lt. Algernon E. Smith, 1st Lt. Donald McIntosh, and Lt. James Calhoun." More than 2,000 members of the post and surrounding community attended the services, which were also reported in the September 8, 1877, issue of *Frank Leslie's Illustrated Newspaper.* (Author's collection and courtesy Library of Congress.)

The c. 1890 photograph above shows the main entrance to the cemetery with the groundskeeper's quarters. Today the cemetery encompasses just over 36 acres, with the remains of 23,000 interred, including eight Medal of Honor recipients and four officers of the U. S. Penitentiary who lost their lives in the line of duty. The cemetery was placed on the National Register of Historic Places on July 15, 1999. (Courtesy Frontier Army Museum.)

During the mid-1800s as photography began capturing events, people, and places, postcards and photograph books became extremely popular and profitable. The above postcard depicts the speaker and bandstand that stood at the National Cemetery. (Courtesy Jim Will.)

The remains of Brig. Gen. Henry Leavenworth were reinterred at the fort during services held on Memorial Day 1902. General Leavenworth died during the Leavenworth-Dodge Expedition of 1834 at Cross Timbers in the Indian Territory of present-day Oklahoma. He was originally buried at Cross Timbers, and his remains were later removed to the Woodland Cemetery in his hometown of New Delphi, New York. This granite marker, topped with an eagle in repose, was erected in 1910. (Courtesy Frontier Army Museum.)

Normandy Chapel sat on Iowa Avenue near the site of the present-day bowling center. This chapel conducted services for Catholic, Mormon, and Protestant soldiers until 1966, when the building was relocated to Third and Kiowa Streets in the city of Leavenworth. (Courtesy Jim Will.)

The main post chapel is located at the corner of Pope and Thomas Avenues. The multi-denominational chapel's opening services were held on January 16, 1969. Margaret Berry, who served as the Memorial Chapel organist from 1930 to 1980, played at the opening services. (Courtesy Frontier Army Museum.)

The interior of the main post chapel is pictured above. The chaplains of the fort have remained committed to providing religious, spiritual, moral, and ethical advice whether it be to the few hundred soldiers of yesterday to the more than 5,000 military service members and their families of today. (Courtesy Frontier Army Museum.)

No better display of community support could surpass the morning of October 27, 2006. The fort showed its love and support for the family of 21-year-old Cpl. David Unger, who succumbed to injuries received when an improvised explosive device detonated near his vehicle while on patrol in Iraq on October 17, 2006. Unger had grown up locally, and by the age of 13 was working at the Main Post Chapel. On a cold and windy morning, the Fort Leavenworth community stood in reverence as the procession entered the reservation escorted by members of the Kansas Patriot Guard, local law enforcement, and military police. The Main Post Chapel was standing room only, and many observers lined the streets as a horse-drawn hearse carried the young soldier to his final resting place. (Courtesy Laura Unger.)

On August 18, 2008, ground was broken for a new post chapel. Dignitaries attending the ceremony were former Kansas representative Nancy Boyda, Missouri representative Ike Skelton, and Texas representative Chet Edwards. Once completed, the 1,191 seat capacity chapel will feature a raised pulpit, choir loft, activity center, and 15 classrooms. A covered walkway will connect the new chapel with the Main Post Chapel. (Courtesy *The Fort Leavenworth Lamp.*)

Seven

U.S. Disciplinary Barracks

In 1871, Brig. Gen. Thomas F. Barr called attention to the conditions in which military prisoners were being confined in 32 different stockades and various state penitentiaries. Punishment varied from institution to institution, and included flogging, ball and chain, shackling, tattooing, branding, solitary confinement, and execution. For his efforts, General Barr would become known as the father of the U.S. military prison. (Courtesy University of Southern California.)

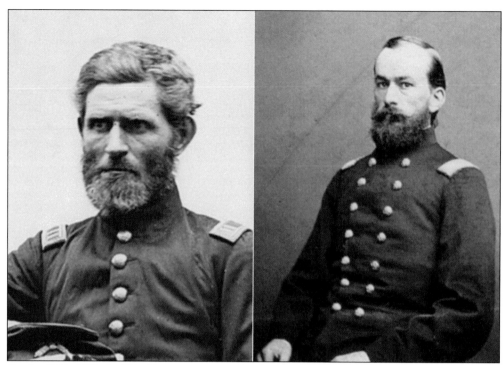

On April 30, 1875, the War Department issued orders designating Maj. James M. Robertson (left) as the prison's first commandment and Capt. Asa P. Blunt (right) as assistant quartermaster in charge of construction. (Author's collection.)

Upon Captain Blunt's arrival, requests for men and materials were submitted and construction began on the high board fence shown in the above photograph. The fence would be completed during the summer of 1875, and renovation of the buildings inside the perimeter began. Inmate labor was used in the renovation and construction process as well as working a 100-acre garden that adjoined the facility. (Courtesy Leavenworth Public Library.)

By the fall of 1876, the inmate population had risen to just over 330 prisoners. A quarry was opened and plans for a permanent wall to replace the wooden fence were drawn up. The plans called for the wall to be 5 feet thick at the base, tapering to 2.5 feet at the top. Construction began in April 1877, and by 1881 the wall was complete. Inmate labor, using rock quarried from the fort, constructed 2,022 feet of wall in just over four years. (Author's collection.)

As the population increased, so did the need for constructive labor. As part of the rehabilitation process, inmates are provided with skills so they may become useful members of society on release. In May 1877, inmates began making boots, shoes, and other leather goods for the quartermaster department. The shoes sold for $1 a pair, and many soldiers found the quality poor. (Author's collection.)

During the first few years of operation, inmates' clothes and linens were laundered outside the institution, but the labor-intensive task of cleaning clothes and returning them to the institution presented many challenges. A building was taken apart outside the walls and reconstructed inside, and the inmate laundry began operation in 1878. (Courtesy Frontier Army Museum.)

Between 1878 and 1880, a chapel was established inside the institution and services were conducted for all faiths and denominations. The chaplains were also given the responsibility of establishing a school. By the end of 1880, a prison library with 667 books was opened. (Courtesy Frontier Army Museum.)

Here is a view of the institution courtyard from the front door of the inmate hospital. Grants for the construction of the first hospital totaled $12,000, and construction began in May 1877. The hospital was located along the original north wall in the area where the front of the Castle once stood. (Courtesy Frontier Army Museum.)

One of the oldest inmate work details was the sheet metal shop, which opened in 1879 and operated until the institution was closed and replaced with the new confinement facility. (Courtesy Frontier Army Museum.)

By the early 1890s, arguments used to open the facility were now being used to close it. The Three Prisons Act of 1893 established the Federal Prison Service, and by 1895 the military handed over control of the facility to the Department of Justice and the first federal penitentiary was established. (Author's collection.)

From the very beginning, the Federal Prison Service determined that the old military prison was not an adequate facility for holding prisoners. In March 1897, construction began on the new U. S. Penitentiary. Inmates would march 3 miles daily at sun up and return just before sundown. By 1906 the institution was completed enough for the old military prison to be returned to the War Department, and once again the U. S. Disciplinary Barracks (USDB) was open for business. (Author's collection.)

Inmate Carl Panzram, pictured during the west wall construction in 1908, was sentenced to two years for stealing clothes from a quartermaster depot. On his release in 1910, Panzram became one of the 20th century's most notorious serial killers, claiming to have committed murders of 21 people and thousands of thefts and arsons. In his autobiography *Killer: A Journal of Murder*, he described himself as "rage personified." While at the federal prison at Leavenworth, Panzram murdered laundry foreman R. G. Warnke in June 1929. He became the first inmate executed at that prison in September 1930. (Author's collection.)

Between 1910 and 1921, construction of the 366,000-square-foot building known as the Castle was underway. Once completed, the institution contained 1,200 cells, 4 cell houses, a dining room, gymnasium, inmate radio station, offices, mail room, library, and death chamber. (Courtesy Frontier Army Museum.)

During the period the USDB served as a federal prison, this stockade was built just northwest of present-day Sherman Army Airfield. This area later operated as the brick factory, quarry, and lime and cement factory. (Courtesy Frontier Army Museum.)

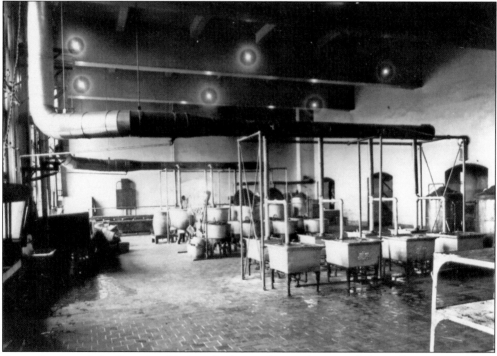

An early view of the five-wing kitchen facility is shown above, and the early prison diet was sparse. Breakfast consisted of a half-pint of milk with 10 ounces of oatmeal or 12 ounces of corn meal. Supper half-pint of milk and 14 ounces of bread. Dinner on Monday, Wednesday, Friday, and Saturday evenings was the same as breakfast. On Tuesdays, Thursdays, and Sundays, dinner was a luxurious 8 ounces of bread and the regular army ration of pork, beans, salt, pepper, and vinegar. Occasionally beef was substituted for pork. Grade one and two inmates could have the same dinner as Thursday on Sunday, with coffee and sugar for breakfast. (Courtesy Frontier Army Museum.)

In the early days of the Castle, inmates all sat facing one direction in total silence in the dining room. (Courtesy Frontier Army Museum.)

This photograph shows an early view of a cell house shortly after the Castle was opened. (Courtesy Frontier Army Museum.)

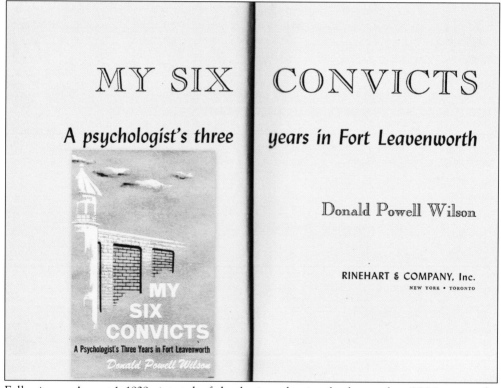

During World War I, the inmate population grew as many Americans drafted claimed conscientious objector status. J. P. Neufeld was a Mennonite received at the USDB on July 25, 1918, on a sentence of 25 years. As the work pass indicates, Neufeld worked nights at the dairy barn. (Author's collection.)

Following an August 1, 1929, riot at the federal prison that involved more than 900 inmates, the USDB was again turned over to the Department of Justice and was known as the Federal Prison Annex until it was returned to military control in 1941. Donald Powell Wilson was a psychologist studying the affects of drugs on criminal behavior and wrote the book *My Six Convicts*, based on his experiences while at the fort. A movie of the same title was released in 1952 and featured Harry Morgan and Charles Bronson in their feature film debuts. (Author's collection.)

The institution's history also includes 29 executions. Between July 10 and August 25, 1945, thirteen men were executed by hanging from an elevator shaft in a warehouse inside the facility. Of those, 12 were German prisoners of war who had murdered fellow countrymen for cooperating with American military officials. Five were granted their last request of being executed wearing their Afrika Korps uniforms. The right photographs show six of the seven German POWs executed on August 25, 1945. (Author's collection.)

Many incidents occur within the walls of any prison that makes headlines. The riot on May 2, 1942, was the result of racial tensions that resulted in the death of one inmate and injuries to six inmates and five guards. Another incident making headlines was the escape on July 25, 1945, when inmates Woodrow Little, Walter Short, and Jose Santelana were being marched outside the walls along with their detail. Suddenly, the trio broke and ran. Pfc. Phillip Koch was on duty in the southwest corner tower and opened fire. Several rounds struck the attendant's car in the filling station (above), and it was also reported that several bullets passed through two homes located at Sumner Place. (Courtesy Robert Beardsley.)

High-profile cases and inmates draw attention to any prison facility. A few examples of high-profile inmates include Thomas R. Barbella (also known as Rocky Graziano), incarcerated for assault and going AWOL; Lt. William Calley incarcerated for his role in the My Lai Massacre; and Marine Sgt. Clayton Lonetree, incarcerated for espionage. Above is a view of the main cell house building known as the Castle. (Courtesy Frontier Army Museum.)

Clayton A. Fountain was sentenced to life for murder, larceny, and robbery. On September 1, 1975, around 11:45 p.m., Fountain took Sgt. Lyn Cox hostage and forced his way into southgate, where he secured a shotgun. Firing shots into the control room (left), Fountain put out an eye of Sgt. Larry Spybuck. The incident ended at 2:30 a.m. after Comdr. Gordon D. Rowe persuaded Fountain to surrender. (Author's collection.)

During the late 1970s and early 1980s, the U.S. Army experimented with and implemented the Special Operations Response Team (SORT) as prison violence began to rise. Soldiers are trained in riot control, hostage extraction, cell extractions, and the use of less lethal munitions. Fashioned after police department SWAT teams, this innovation to corrections would soon be adopted by all correctional departments worldwide. (Author's collection.)

In September 2002, inmates from the old USDB were moved into a new 500-man-capacity institution located on land that used to occupy the institution's farm operation. The modern facility provides for greater security and safety of the staff and inmates. Its open design provides greater visibility for custody and control of the modern inmate population. (Author's collection.)

Though there were efforts to save the Castle by many, the military concluded that the facility was too structurally unsound and too extensive to renovate. Demolition began in 2004 and took a few months to complete. (Author's collection.)

All that remains of the old military prison today are a few old buildings, the wall, and a parking lot where the Castle once stood. (Author's collection.)

Eight

HOUSE OF GENERALS

In 1881, Commanding General of the Army William T. Sherman (right), along with other military reformers, believed that the military was changing in tactics and organization due to modern technology. His belief was that modern officers could not rely on the "school of war" for their education and that an advanced professional education of officers was needed. Calling on his experience as the superintendent of the Louisiana State Seminary of Learning and Military Academy, General Sherman ordered the establishment of the School of Application for Cavalry and Infantry on May 7, 1881. (Courtesy Library of Congress.)

MAJ. GEN. ELWELL S. OTIS.

The first commandant of the school was Col. Elwell S. Otis, who had gained considerable experience during the Civil War and numerous skirmishes with Native Americans. The teaching cadre consisted of two majors and three captains, only one of whom had any teaching experience. (Courtesy Library of Congress.)

When the class of 1883 arrived, many obstacles confronted them. Textbooks were in short supply and the library existed in name only. Colonel Otis had requested $5,000 for books, maps, and other instructional supplies and was granted only $500. (Courtesy Combined Arms Research Library.)

Because so many of the young officers sent to the class came from varied educational backgrounds, they had to be placed in two separate classes. The first class studied tactics, organization, drill, and other military subjects. The second class studied reading, writing, arithmetic, trigonometry, and history. Many commanding officers regarded the school so poorly that they only sent their less experienced junior grade officers. (Courtesy Combined Arms Research Library.)

Two instructors who would leave an indelible mark on the school's success were Eben Swift (left) and Arthur L. Wagner (right). Together they developed courses of study, wrote curriculum, and produced textbooks. Both drew heavily on military history to prepare operational orders and procedures for the order of combat. The orders included information on the situation, objective, disposition of troops, assignments, logistics, and combat communications. They are remembered as pioneers of American military education. (Courtesy Library of Congress.)

Between 1898 and 1902, operations at the school were suspended due the Spanish-American War. From 1903 to 1906, Maj. Gen. James Franklin Bell (above) was commandant of the Infantry and Cavalry School. Bell's forceful and progressive leadership expanded the curriculum and called for officers to observe a corps, division, or brigade organized and on the march. Bell believed this method would better prepare officers in the performance of their duties. He became known as the father of the Leavenworth schools. (Courtesy author's collection.)

At 25 years of age, Lt. George C. Marshall was the youngest officer in his class. The photograph at left was taken in 1907, shortly after he graduated first in his class. After graduating at the top of his class again in 1908, Marshall remained at the college as an instructor (right). He would later write of his Leavenworth experience, "To become a Leavenworth man was a prestigious mark of success without which no officer could aspire to future high command or compete for the few high positions in the peacetime army." (Courtesy Frontier Army Museum.)

Barth Hall was the original home of the School of Application for Cavalry and Infantry in 1881, and now houses the headquarters of the Battle Command Training Program. (Courtesy Combined Arms Research Library.)

By 1908, the Army Service School included a school for engineers. One of the earliest instructors of the school, Lt. Douglas MacArthur (sitting on handrail) came to Fort Leavenworth seeking command experience, and served as troop commander and adjutant. Shortly after the death of his father, MacArthur's mother lived with the young lieutenant in his quarters at the Rookery. (Courtesy Frontier Army Museum.)

The engineer school included the building of bridges and the use of explosives. (Courtesy Frontier Army Museum.)

Engineers cross Merritt Lake via the pontoon bridge they constructed. The lake honors Maj. Gen. Wesley Merritt, a distinguished Cavalry officer whose career spanned 40 years and three wars. Major General Merritt served as Department of the Missouri commander at Fort Leavenworth from 1887 to 1890. (Courtesy Frontier Army Museum.)

This engineers' tool wagon sits in front of the U.S. Engineer Depot. Today the location is an indoor riding area located north of the stables. (Courtesy Frontier Army Museum.)

Though he was not a graduate of the Leavenworth schools, Gen. John J. Pershing (seen above in downtown Leavenworth shortly after World War I) cherished the values of a professional military education. In July 1917, while establishing his headquarters in Chaumont, France, Pershing requested 27 officers whom he believed were best suited for staff duty. All army, corps, and divisional levels command positions Pershing staffed throughout Europe were filled with Leavenworth graduates. (Courtesy Frontier Army Museum.)

Following World War I, the schools reopened as the General Service Schools in 1919. This included the School of the Line, General Staff School, and Signal Corps School. The left photograph is of an army dirigible used during training by the signal corps. Dirigibles such as these were used for aerial reconnaissance and photography. (Courtesy Frontier Army Museum.)

The above photograph shows a U.S. Army Signal Corps School class in telegraphy around 1919. (Courtesy Frontier Army Museum.)

George S. Patton (left), class of 1924, would give this advice to officers attending the school: "When at the school study hard but not excessively. I studied every evening from seven to eleven. If I was through at that time I went to bed, if I finished earlier I also went to bed and did not devil myself with extra work. On Friday after the map problem, I went home and took several big drinks to relax my mind." Patton finished in the top 25 percent of his class. Patton also provided copies of his notes to students such as Dwight D. Eisenhower (right), class of 1926. Patton would often tease Eisenhower about finishing at the top of the class using his notes. (Author's collection.)

By 1922, the school began an educational program for the National Guard and reserves. Instructors provided training at reserve summer camps and a correspondence course was developed for the officers of the National Guard and reserves as well as selected civilians. The War Department also convened a board of officers that would recommend changes to the school. Their findings included recommendations for shortening the school from two years to one and changing the name of the school to the Command and General Staff School. (Courtesy Frontier Army Museum.)

From 1931 to 1940, the 1st Squad of the 10th U.S. Cavalry functioned as support troops for the CGSC. (Courtesy Frontier Army Museum.)

With the outbreak of World War II, there was a greater demand for graduates than ever before. Brig. Gen. Leslie J. McNair, the school's commandant, reorganized the school to meet the demand. McNair doubled the size of classes and an accelerated version of the regular course of study was begun. Two classes of four and a half months replaced the class of 1940–1941. As the need for officers increased, this class was reduced to a nine-week course of studies. These first classes were comprised of officers of the National Guard, reserves, and a small contingency of regular U.S. Army. (Author's collection.)

WAAC OFFICERS GO TO THE SCHOOL OF WAR

The WAAC Officers have finished their first 10 weeks course and all graduated from the toughest military school in the United States, I won't say the world, The Command and General Staff School at Fort Leavenworth, Kansas, which proves their capability. This is the first time in the history of the school women were admitted to any of its courses, and know of no woman ever to attend even one class.

As World War II continued into 1943, all able-bodied men were needed for the war effort. That year's class included for the first time female officers of the Women's Army Auxiliary Corps. Capt. Elizabeth Cartwright Rudd recalls, "We learned unusual things. One of the classes was a class in the tactics that were used at Gettysburg, and how that is classic military tactics everybody in the army should know . . . We trained to be adjutants to work with some colonel somewhere helping him run the supply department." The news article and interview shown above are the only known records of that first class. (Courtesy the Combined Arms Research Library and Library of Congress.)

As World War II unfolded, the school adapted to organizational and technical demands as they developed, and met the challenge of new practices and problems as they emerged on the battlefield. Instructors rewrote curriculum, ushering in the new and eliminating the old. They ensured their students carried with them knowledge and education that would make them effective leaders not only on the battlefield, but also during their peacetime assignments. The view above is a classroom in Gruber Hall (Courtesy Frontier Army Museum.)

In keeping pace with the war, the school's liaison officer received news from the battlefields of Europe and the Pacific daily, and immediately incorporated it into the course of study. Information was also gathered as the school sent officers to tour battlefields to obtain valuable first-hand knowledge. Secretary of War Henry L. Stimson wrote in his memoirs, "The staff work of the American army came of age in World War II. What brilliant individuals had done in earlier wars was done this time by thousands of officers trained in the maturing traditions of Leavenworth." (Author's collection.)

The cold war era would present issues and demand more of the college than ever before. This was a period of dynamic growth and change. The curriculum incorporated to courses in nuclear weapons. Limited and counterinsurgency warfare, as well as major tactical reorganization of the U.S. Army, kept students and staff busy. Above is a typical classroom in Muir Hall. (Courtesy Frontier Army Museum.)

By the end of the 1950s, the expansion of the curriculum demanded growth of the college. Ground was broken on Arsenal Hill for the construction of J. Franklin Bell Hall on November 6, 1956, and the building was dedicated on 14 January 1959. Pres. Dwight D. Eisenhower wrote, "This building stands as a strong sign that the Command and General Staff College will continue to train leaders to meet the challenges of the future." (Courtesy Frontier Army Museum.)

With the addition of Bell Hall, the students' focus was directed toward an increase in flexible response, with greater emphasis on conventional forces and limited wars. The class of 1959–1960 numbered approximately 1,200 students. Officers of the U.S. Army, Air Force, Marines, and Navy, as well as approximately 150 Allied officers from 43 countries were in attendance. (Courtesy Frontier Army Museum.)

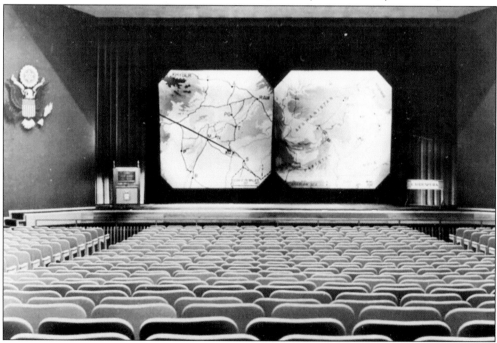

Eisenhower auditorium inside Bell Hall provided space for meetings, guest speakers, classroom instruction, and graduation facilities. Members of the fort and the local community also used the auditorium for various other functions. (Courtesy Frontier Army Museum.)

With the opening of Bell Hall, CGSC provided extension courses in which nearly 15,000 officers enrolled the first year. They included U.S. Army Reserve associate CGSC courses, reserve component staff training, and nuclear weapons refresher Courses. Above is a view of the Archives Reading Room of the Combined Arms Research Library. (Courtesy Frontier Army Museum.)

In 1962, the U.S. Army began its master of military art and science degree program. After the Vietnam War, the college curriculum continued to develop and change. Theories of the central battle, fight outnumbered and win, the integrated battlefield, rapid deployment, and the Army 86 doctrine all challenged the faculty and students, testing and demanding their best. (Courtesy Frontier Army Museum.)

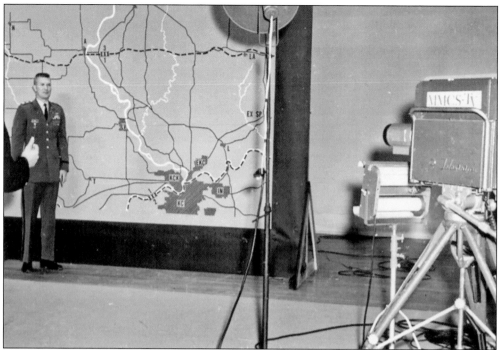

MMCS television in the late 1960s provided teleconferencing capabilities throughout J. Franklin Bell Hall. It could also provide closed-circuit information to all military personnel and their families throughout the post. (Courtesy Frontier Army Museum.)

Throughout the school's history, many international military students have attended classes. The first international student arrived in 1894 from the Swiss army and completed a six-month course of study. The first international member of the faculty was Lt. Col. G. Peron of the French army in 1921. Today international students from 45 countries attend classes at the college. (Courtesy Combined Arms Research Library.)

The Command and General Staff College continues to evolve. On July 1, 2004, ground was broken for the new Lewis and Clark Center. This 410,000-square foot, $115 million state-of-the-art facility features 96 classrooms and can accommodate more than 1,500 resident students. (Author's collection.)

Each classroom accommodates 16 students. Features include disappearing computer monitors that are hooked up to remote units so no computers take up valuable workspace, two 65-inch plasma displays, and cameras so each classroom can conduct video teleconferencing. (Author's collection.)

The center includes two auditoriums. The Eisenhower Auditorium has a capacity of 2,004, with full stage lighting, a state-of-the-art large screen projection system, and audio system. The Marshall Auditorium accommodates 325 people and includes video teleconferencing capabilities. It may be used for conferences, formal meetings and includes computer stations and microphones. A cafeteria services the school and features a Subway, Einstein Bagels, Anthony's Pizza, and Charlie's Sandwiches. The center also includes a popular bookstore known throughout the world, which offers the largest collections of military-oriented books anywhere. (Author's collection.)

Moving forward but never forgetting its past, today's Command and General Staff College remains dedicated to providing a world-class professional military education, challenging students to solve complex problems in an ever-changing world. The school instills core values of service to the nation, loyalty, duty, respect, selfless service, honor, integrity, and personnel courage. (Author's collection.)

Nine

THROUGH THE YEARS

Standing at the intersection of Arsenal (present-day Scott) and Pope Avenues, this Iron Gate, erected in the late 1850s, was the original front entrance to Fort Leavenworth. Some of the most important figures in U.S. Army history have passed through these gates. No story should ever be told about the West that does not include the contributions of Fort Leavenworth or the soldiers who forged the frontier. Their devotion to duty still echoes through the community today, forever linking the past to the present. (Courtesy Frontier Army Museum.)

To the left of the photograph is the arsenal. The right-hand fork leads to the city of Leavenworth. (Courtesy Frontier Army Museum.)

No. 203 Meade Avenue was constructed around 1859, and served as quarters for the ordnance detachment. It has also served as the office of the depot quartermaster. In 1915, this building was renovated as quarters for noncommissioned officers. (Courtesy Frontier Army Museum.)

No. 1 Scott Avenue was built around 1861 on land originally set aside as the soldiers' cemetery. It has served as a residence for the arsenal, departmental, and post commanders. Legend persists that the quarters are haunted by the spirit of George Armstrong Custer, who purportedly spent several evenings here before departing for the Little Big Horn Valley, where he took his place in history. (Courtesy Frontier Army Museum.)

FUNSTON FIRES ON BURGLAR.

Intruder In His Room Had Fired First —Neither Hit.

LEAVENWORTH, Kan., June 7.—Brig. Gen. Frederick Funston, Commandant of the army service schools at Fort Leavenworth, engaged in a revolver fight with a supposed burglar in his quarters at the post early to-day. The man escaped and Gen. Funston was unharmed.

Gen. Funston had gone to bed late. He lay awake in bed for an hour. Then a closet door opened and a man stepped forth. The General saw him and reached under his pillow for a revolver. The intruder saw the motion and fired. The bullet pierced the mattress near the General, who leaped to his feet. He turned on the lights and fired three shots as the man fled.

" I believe he was a burglar," said Gen. Funston, " waiting until I was asleep to rifle my pockets."

On the evening of June 7, 1909, Brig. Gen. Frederick Funston returned to his quarters at No. 1 Scott Avenue and encountered what appeared to be a burglar. As the newspaper clipping indicates, neither man was a crack shot. (Author's collection.)

This *c.* 1872 view faces south along Arsenal (present-day Scott) Avenue. The one-story building to the left is the original post office. Located directly north of 612 Scott Avenue, this building was originally constructed of logs in 1835, and has served as the residence for post chaplains, staff officers, and aides to departmental commanders. This building was torn down and the post office was relocated to Boughton Hall in 1923. (Courtesy Frontier Army Museum.)

This house on 611 Scott Avenue, built around 1841, was originally constructed of hand-hewn logs. Though much of the original structure still exists, it is mostly concealed behind walls and partitions. The home has undergone several renovations and enlargements through the years, and has served as the residence of the post sutler and department and post commanders. It was in this home that the first governor of Kansas took his meals with post sutler Hiram Rich. It was also home to Brig. Gen. Colin Powell from 1980 to 1981. (Courtesy Frontier Army Museum.)

Since 1833 many different stables have existed on the fort. The first were built along the south side of Sumner Place and were later torn down. In 1855 a set of 10 stables were built along the north end of McClelland Avenue. They were destroyed by fire in 1873. The brick stables such as the one pictured above were built in 1893 and have served many purposes through the years. (Courtesy Frontier Army Museum.)

The building at 16–18 Sumner Place was built around 1886 and is another set of quarters purportedly haunted. The legend of the lady in the black dress began in 1975, when a young boy spoke of a ghost reading him stories at bedtime. Scared off one evening by the boy's parents, she traveled next door, where she turns lights on and off and rattles doorknobs. She even helped out the weary housewife by scraping and stacking the dinner dishes while the family was away. This prompted the housewife to lament, "If your quarters have to have a ghost it might as well do the dishes on occasion." (Courtesy Frontier Army Museum.)

On July 20, 1868, Congress approved the construction of a bridge spanning the Missouri River from Fort Leavenworth to Weston, Missouri. Nicknamed the "Whiskey Bridge," the $750,000 combination railroad, transit, and wagon bridge opened for business on April 10, 1872. It was used by the Chicago, Rock Island, and Pacific Railroad as well as the Great Western Railway until 1893. By the 1930s, all rail traffic had ceased. The bridge was renovated and used by the inmates of the federal prison who worked on the prison farm. The bridge would remain in service until 1955, when the new Centennial Bridge replaced it. Demolition of the old bridge began in November 1963. (Courtesy Frontier Army Museum.)

This photograph shows a scenic view of the bridge. (Courtesy Combined Arms Research Library.)

Railroad service on the fort was established in 1870, and the train station above was built in 1903. Railroad companies providing service included the Chicago, Rock Island and Pacific; Fort Leavenworth Railroad Company; Missouri Pacific; Atchison, Topeka, and Santa Fe; and Union Pacific. (Courtesy Frontier Army Museum.)

The first rapid transit line was established in 1888 along the west side of Grant Avenue, linking the fort and downtown Leavenworth. The fare was 10¢ one way, and 15¢ for a round trip. (Courtesy Frontier Army Museum.)

Originally constructed as a waiting room for the trolley, this building was renovated in 1930 and used as the post exchange. In 1937, a south wing was added that included a barbershop, restaurant, and office. (Courtesy Frontier Army Museum.)

Shortly after the death of Ulysses S. Grant, Gen. Nelson A. Miles received a proposal calling for the construction of a statue commemorating the Civil War general and president. The Hodges and McCarthy Monument builders of St. Louis secured the talent of artist Loredo Taft to create the monument. Dedication ceremonies were held on September 14, 1889, and were attended by 10,000 people, including Sen. John J. Ingalls, U.S. Attorney George R. Peck, with the unveiling by Gen. Wesley Merritt. The total cost of the statue was $4,791.61. (Courtesy Frontier Army Museum.)

The original post hospital was located on Thomas Avenue on the site of the former officers' club. Two other hospitals were built in 1833 and 1902. A women's ward was added in 1910, and the hospital featured a solarium, passageway, and a double deck runway. (Courtesy Frontier Army Museum.)

Located on Pope Avenue, Munson Army Hospital opened in May 1960, and was named for Brig. Gen. Edward L. Munson (inset), founder of the Medical Field Services School at Fort Leavenworth in 1910. (Courtesy Frontier Army Museum.)

The first post school, located south of 605 Scott Avenue, was built by Post Sutler Goodfellow, whose wife and daughters resided in and operated the school. It was torn down in 1917. (Courtesy Frontier Army Museum.)

In March 1901, Fort Leavenworth was organized as a separate school district from the County of Leavenworth. Prior to this date, fort children were charged a tuition fee to attend the public school system. This second post school, above, was constructed in 1914 along Scott Avenue just south of Riverside Apartments. (Courtesy Frontier Army Museum.)

As the post has grown, so has its school system. In 1953, Gen. Dwight D. Eisenhower Elementary opened, followed in 1956 by Gen. Douglas MacArthur Elementary. The above photograph shows Gen. Omar N. Bradley during opening ceremonies for a school named in his honor. A middle school is named in honor of Gen. George S. Patton Jr. (Courtesy Frontier Army Museum.)

On October 23, 1907, the YMCA building was dedicated. Helen Miller Gould and Chaplain John T. Axton attended the ceremonies. Gould was the daughter of railroad tycoon Jay Gould, and donated $50,000 for the construction and furnishing of the building. Chaplain Axton had taken up the task started by Chaplain John S. Randolph, petitioning for and overseeing the construction. In 1955, the building was renovated and renamed in honor of Gen. Alexander M. Patch. (Courtesy Frontier Army Museum.)

Shortly after the fort was established, a rough stone wall was erected on a knoll just south of the encampment as protection from possible Native American attacks. Eventually the wall developed into a looped wall in which a blockhouse stood. In 1903, when the old dragoon barracks were torn down, it was suggested that the wall be removed. (Courtesy Frontier Army Museum.)

The wall was saved and restored through the efforts of the Daughters of the American Revolution. The above photograph was taken during the dedication ceremonies in 1917. (Courtesy Frontier Army Museum.)

Originally constructed in 1882 to house a small regiment of infantry, this building has been the home of the post headquarters, regimental band, and a regiment of engineers. From 1901 to 1909, four wings were added, as well as a third floor. In 1921, the building was renovated to accommodate 48 officers and their families. Housing more than 2,600 families between 1921 and 1978, this building became known as the "Beehive" because it was buzzing with activity. The building was vacant from 1978 to 1993 and now serves as the home of the National Simulation Center. (Courtesy Frontier Army Museum.)

Constructed as officers' quarters in 1886, this building was located on McClelland Avenue and was later occupied by the officers' club. The officers' club relocated to what is now the Frontier Conference Center. (Courtesy Frontier Army Museum.)

The troops of the engineers' barracks enjoy their off-duty time. (Courtesy Frontier Army Museum.)

Built in 1892, Pope Hall was located on Scott Avenue directly across from the main entrance to the old military prison. It has served as a dance hall, recreation hall, post school, chapel, and golf club. The building was also equipped with a full stage for the presentation of plays. In May 1957, this building was destroyed by fire while it was being used for instruction in the tactical deployment of nuclear weapons. (Courtesy Frontier Army Museum.)

The Army Air Corps developed Sherman Army Airfield in 1923 under the jurisdiction of the old military prison. The original 1,800-foot runway was built in the middle of an alfalfa field and was intended for emergency landings. Named in honor of Maj. William C. Sherman, an early army aviation pioneer, the airfield occupies land where Chief Joseph and Nez Perce were held after their surrender to Gen. Nelson A. Miles in October 1877. As early as 1839, the area was also the site of a racetrack where cavalry horses were tested as well as a site for skeet shooting. During World War II, members of the National Guard and units of Dutch East Indies Air Force trained here. After the development of the U.S. Air Force, the field was operated as Sherman Air Force Base. (Courtesy Frontier Army Museum.)

In 1920, Congress approved the National Defense Act as a measure to prepare for the nation's military readiness. Civilian Military Training Camps were established as an introduction to military training for young men of high school and college age intent on preparing them for reserve or National Guard duty. The above photograph shows CMTC students being issued the oath in August 1926. (Courtesy Frontier Army Museum.)

The post theater was dedicated on August 14, 1938 and was named The War Department Theater. Besides showing motion pictures, this theater has also been used for graduation ceremonies, guest speakers, special appearances, concerts, and plays. (Courtesy Frontier Army Museum.)

A view of the theater lobby on opening night reveals the weekend's films: *Bulldog Drummond's Revenge* starring John Barrymore was Friday's feature, *Wide Open Faces* featuring Joe E. Brown was shown Saturday, and *Bluebeard's 8th Wife* with Claudette Colbert and Gary Cooper wrapped up the weekend. (Frontier Army Museum.)

With the outbreak of World War II, Fort Leavenworth was once again called on to serve as reception center and training post. A series of 16 postcards chronicled the soldiers' training. The training area and barracks were located in the area of the present-day commissary, post exchange, bowling center, and Harney Gym. (Courtesy Jim Will.)

On July 22, 1958, a ground-breaking ceremony was held that signaled change had once again come not only to this small frontier post, but to the rest of the world as well. Shortly thereafter, construction began on the Nike Hercules Defense System, signaling Fort Leavenworth's entry into the Cold War. (Courtesy Frontier Army Museum.)

The scene portrayed in this photograph seems more like the set of *Dr. Strangelove* than the command center for D Battery, 5th Missile Battalion, 55th Artillery. (Courtesy Frontier Army Museum.)

As early as 1924, efforts were undertaken to establish a post museum in an attempt to preserve the artifacts that were located all over the fort. The museum was formally established in 1938, and was originally located on McPherson Avenue, Bluntville Loop. It moved to its current location in Andrews Hall in 1959. (Courtesy Frontier Army Museum.)

Located along the west side of Grant Avenue was a former consolidated mess hall that was converted into the post commissary. The right photograph was taken during opening day ceremonies in 1952. (Courtesy Frontier Army Museum.)

This post exchange service station was located east of Funston Hall in what is now a parking lot. (Courtesy Frontier Army Museum.)

Today a new commissary and post exchange complex provides one central location for the post community. Goods and services available range from groceries, dry cleaners, banking facilities, a food court, and a vehicle service center. (Courtesy author's collection.)

Many different organizations provide activities for fort youth. Pictured above is the Girl Scout Tandem Drill Team. Boy and Girl Scout troops were organized at the fort in the 1920s and still exist today. (Courtesy Frontier Army Museum.)

In 1926, the Hunt was organized, and in 1931 the organization officially became a member of the National Steeplechase and Hunt Association but disbanded during World War II. In 1951, the Fort Leavenworth Riding Association group was formed. In 1966, the Masters of Fox Hounds Association of America recognized the group's activities as an official hunt. (Courtesy Frontier Army Museum.)

This specially designed bandwagon joined the foxhunt festivities during the early years. The hunts are organized for every level of riding experience, with hunting season between October and April. Today's hunts are for chase only, and even include a guided group known as hilltoppers, who follow along at a slower pace without jumps. (Courtesy Frontier Army Museum.)

This postcard view shows the clubhouse at the Trails West Golf Course. One of the early patrons who learned the game of golf here was then Maj. Dwight Eisenhower who was attending classes at the college in 1925–1926. (Courtesy Jim Will.)

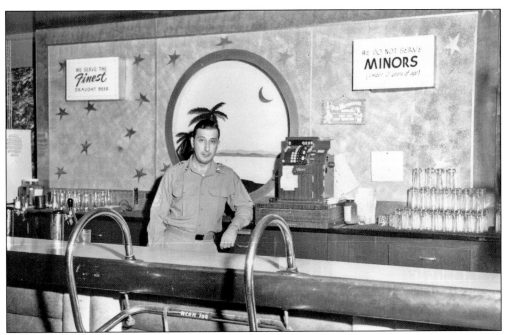

The NCO Club was located on Grant Avenue just south of the post theater. This interior view of the bar was taken in 1958. This building was torn down during a renovation and construction project in the late 1980s and was eventually replaced by the Havana Beach Club. (Courtesy Frontier Army Museum.)

Passing through these front gates today are the military men and women whose legacy has yes yet to be written. One day another author will write of them as many have written of those who have passed this way before. For the past 182 years, the soldiers of Fort Leavenworth and their families have formed a community that reaches far beyond the confines of this frontier post, holding onto their history of the past and embracing the history of their future with an ever-steadfast devotion to duty and undeniable love of country. (Author's collection.)

DISCOVER THOUSANDS OF LOCAL HISTORY BOOKS
FEATURING MILLIONS OF VINTAGE IMAGES

Arcadia Publishing, the leading local history publisher in the United States, is committed to making history accessible and meaningful through publishing books that celebrate and preserve the heritage of America's people and places.

Find more books like this at
www.arcadiapublishing.com

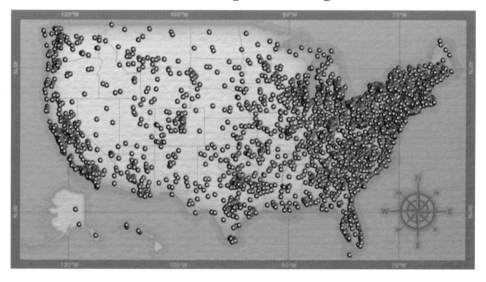

Search for your hometown history, your old stomping grounds, and even your favorite sports team.